How do make paper?

Contents

Written by Sarah Jane Lewis-Mantzaris

Illustrated by Emily Hunter-Higgins

Collins

What's in this book?

Listen and say

trees

paper newspaper

cardboard

"How do you make a book?" asked Nina.

"From paper," said her dad.

4

Chapter 1 How do we use paper?

We use paper every day.

There's paper in our homes, schools and shops.

There's paper in our books and in our toys and games.

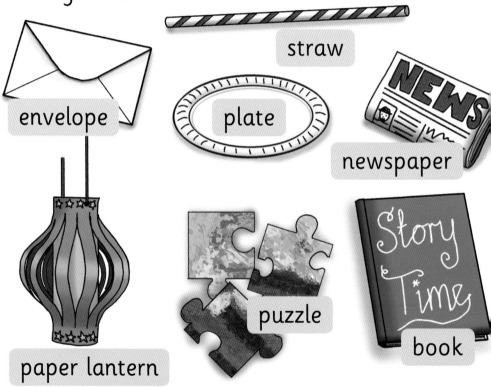

straw

envelope

plate

newspaper

paper lantern

puzzle

book

Can you see any paper where you are now?

Some paper is thin. We use paper tissues for our noses.

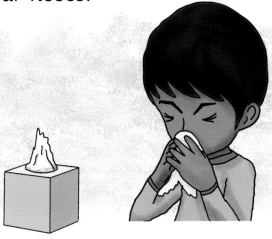

Some paper is hard and strong. This is cardboard. Some boxes are made with cardboard and make things safe.

Chapter 2 How do we make paper?

Look at those trees!

trees in a forest

Paper starts in a forest. Paper is made from trees. There are young trees growing next to old ones. We cut down trees to make paper, and we plant new ones.

People cut down the big trees and cut them into logs. Trucks take the logs to a paper factory.

In a paper factory, they take the bark off the logs. They crush the trees with a big machine to make fibres. They mix the fibres with water and make pulp.

logs

bark

crushing machine

They take out the water and dry the paper flat with hot air. Then the paper is rolled up ready to go to the shop.

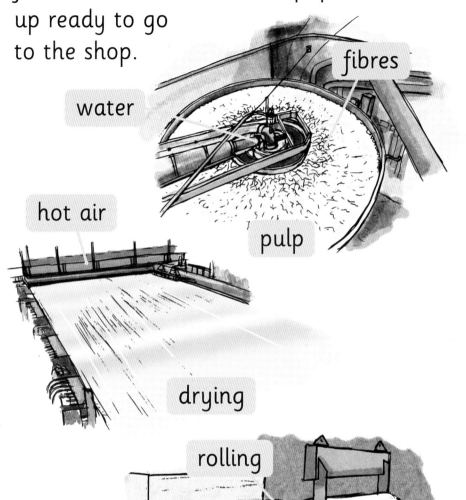

fibres

water

hot air

pulp

drying

rolling

Chapter 3 Different ways to make paper

Paper is very old. In China, a man named Cai Lun made the first paper. He cut some bamboo. Then he added the fibres to water. He dried them on old clothes and had the first paper.

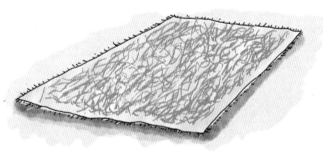

The word *paper* comes from the word
papyrus. Papyrus is a plant. A long time
ago in Egypt, people used papyrus to
make paper.

Today, we can make paper in different ways. In some countries, they make paper from elephant dung. Elephants eat lots of plants, so their dung is full of fibre. And it doesn't smell!

Chapter 4 Recycling paper

We throw away lots of paper and card.

We use about 12 million tonnes of paper every year. That is a lot of trees.

We can recycle paper to make new things. In seven days, an old newspaper can make a new newspaper. Each tonne of recycled paper saves 17 trees!

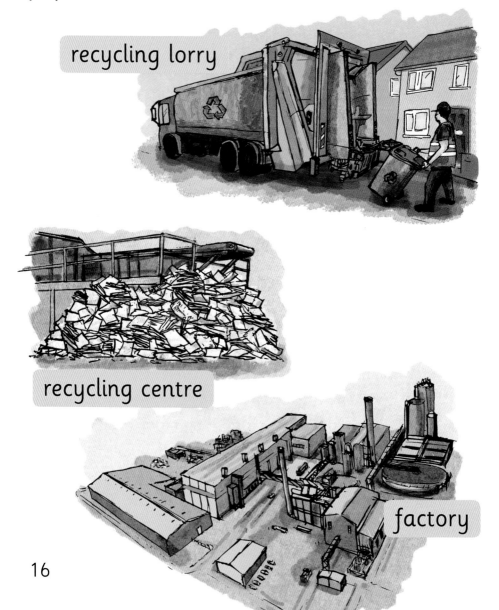

recycling lorry

recycling centre

factory

paper fibres

Do you recycle your paper?

We can recycle paper five times.
Recycled paper makes:

toilet paper

cardboard

food boxes

drawing paper

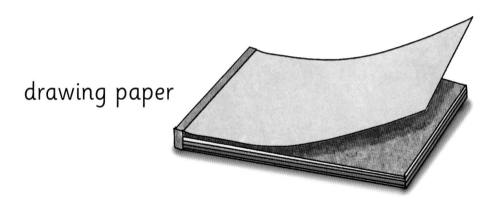

paper for presents

paper logs

Chapter 5 Great things made from paper

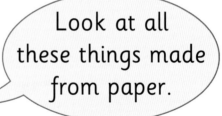

Look at all these things made from paper.

Paper sculptures

Origami

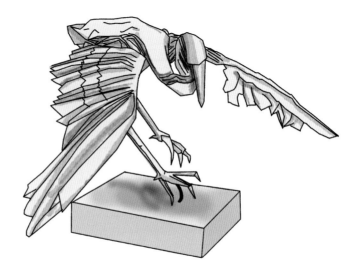

Paper planes

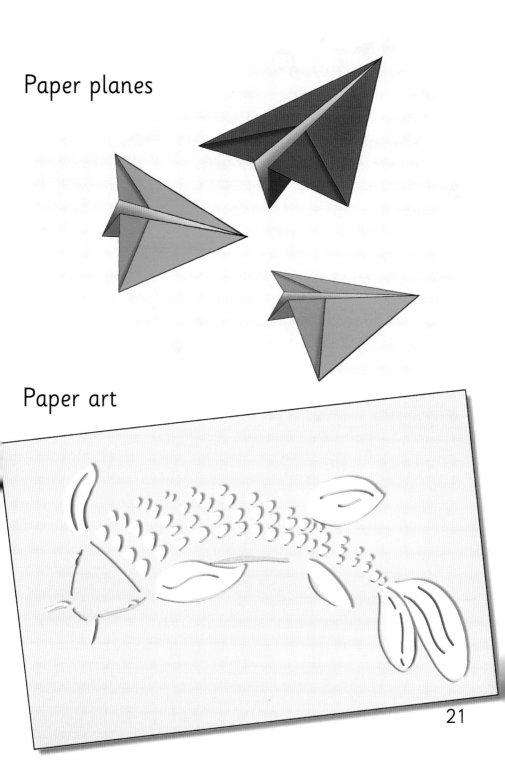

Paper art

Picture dictionary

Listen and repeat

bamboo   bark   cut down

dung   factory   fibres   growing

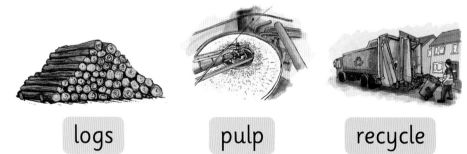

logs   pulp   recycle

1 Look and order

 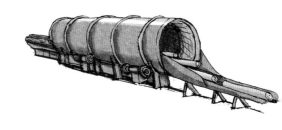

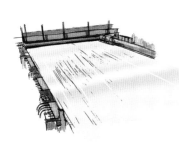 

2 Listen and say

Collins

Published by Collins
An imprint of HarperCollins*Publishers*
Westerhill Road
Bishopbriggs
Glasgow
G64 2QT

HarperCollins*Publishers*
1st Floor, Watermarque Building
Ringsend Road
Dublin 4
Ireland

William Collins' dream of knowledge for all began with the publication of his first book in 1819.

A self-educated mill worker, he not only enriched millions of lives, but also founded a flourishing publishing house. Today, staying true to this spirit, Collins books are packed with inspiration, innovation and practical expertise. They place you at the centre of a world of possibility and give you exactly what you need to explore it.

© HarperCollins*Publishers* Limited 2020

10 9 8 7 6 5 4 3 2

ISBN 978-0-00-839643-5

Collins® and COBUILD® are registered trademarks of HarperCollins*Publishers* Limited

www.collins.co.uk/elt

British Library Cataloguing in Publication Data

A catalogue record for this publication is available from the British Library.

Author: Sarah Jane Lewis-Mantzaris
Illustrator: Emily Hunter-Higgins (Beehive)
Series editor: Rebecca Adlard
Commissioning editor: Zoë Clarke
Publishing manager: Lisa Todd
Product managers: Jennifer Hall and Caroline Green
In-house editor: Alma Puts Keren
Project manager: Emily Hooton
Editor: Frances Amrani
Proofreaders: Natalie Murray and Michael Lamb
Cover designer: Kevin Robbins
Typesetter: 2Hoots Publishing Services Ltd
Audio produced by id audio, London
Reading guide author: Emma Wilkinson
Production controller: Rachel Weaver
Printed and bound by: GPS Group, Slovenia

Download the audio for this book and a reading guide for parents and teachers at www.collins.co.uk/839643